My New Life: A Handbook for Born-again Believers

REV. LINDA SEATTS-OGLETREE

Copyright © 2017 Linda Seatts-Ogletree

All rights reserved.

ISBN-13: 978-0-9990556-0-1
Kittrell Publishing House • P.O. Box 760157 • Lathrup Village, MI 48076

DEDICATION

I dedicate this book in memory of my parents, Lowell and Lillian Massey, my husband, Richard, my son Anthony K. Seatts, II, Daughter, Lauren Seatts, Max and Ava.

CONTENTS

	Acknowledgments	i
1	Introduction	1
2	Now that you are a Born-again Believer	9
3	The Holy Spirit & Baptism	26
4	Joy, Trials & Tribulations	33
5	Read & Study the Word of God	44
6	How to Pray	49
7	Faith, Obedience & Witness	55
8	Praise, Worship & Spiritual Gifts	64
9	Church Fellowship & Saved to Serve	71
10	Spiritual Growth is a Process	77
	About the Author	80
	Appendix	83
	The Holy Trinity	84
	Bibliography	87

ACKNOWLEDGMENTS

I am thankful to my professors at Ashland Theological Seminary who equipped me with the knowledge to teach and preach the gospel of Jesus Christ. I am grateful to all my spiritual mentors, the late Pastor Alexander D. Wright, Bishop Millicent Thompson, Rev. "Dr." Jessica Ingram, and Pastor Solomon W. Kinloch, who showed me how to be an authentic minister of the Gospel. I acknowledge my biggest supporters, husband Richard, my son Anthony K. Seatts, II and my fellow brothers & sisters in Christ.

CHAPTER 1
INTRODUCTION

My New Life handbook endeavors to offer believers an overview of what it truly means to be a "born-again Christian and live a victorious life. ***My New Life*** is not an "academic" book; it is a biblical practical guide written in simple terms that are applicable to your daily life.

Many times, new believers in Christ don't know what it means to be a Christian. I wish I had a handbook like this when I was born-again. It would have helped me manage my new life much better. However, the beauty behind life's challenges is the indwelling power of the Holy Spirit that will help you overcome each challenge. You now have the Father, Son and Holy Ghost on your side, a powerful trinity that no man, woman, or situation can come up against.

My New Life is a simple, easy-to-read book that will enlighten born-again believers that being "saved" doesn't mean life is going to be free of challenges, trouble, and problems. However, as a born-again believer in Christ you have access to El Shaddai, the Lord God Almighty, and surely, He's able to provide you with everything you need for a victorious life.

Throughout this handbook, you will

discover the Word of God-the Holy Bible, is alive and powerful! ***My New Life*** will show you how the Word of God can keep you sane and victorious in this sin-sick world. If God is for you, who can be against you?

It is our hope that after you read this book, your hunger and thirst will intensify for studying and meditating upon God's Word. May God bless and keep you on this awesome journey of victory and freedom in Jesus Christ.

"In the beginning, God created the heavens and the earth." Genesis 1:1.

God created a perfect, holy world without sin. He created man and woman in His image. God didn't manufacture us to be programmed robots. He created us with spirit, body, and soul! When God created us, He gave us the capacity of "free will" --the ability to make choices.

However, something happened in the Garden of Eden. Adam and Eve, the first man and woman--the first parents of humanity, was tempted by the serpent, which is the devil. By allowing the devil to tempt them, they disobeyed God and chose to eat from the Tree of the Knowledge of Good and Evil, a tree God specifically instructed them not to eat from or else they would die (**Genesis 2:15-17**). Once Adam and Eve ate the fruit from the forbidden tree, they disobeyed God. Therefore, disobedience was the first sin that entered the world.

The entrance of sin into the world altered the original creation and therefore, death became the penalty for sin.

Because God loved us so much, He gave us another chance through His grace (love) and mercy (compassion). God's love gave us another opportunity to live through spiritual rebirth. According to **John 3:5,** we can be born-again and live a new life.

God offered His Son, Jesus the Christ as the ultimate sacrifice. Jesus took all our sins--past, present, and future--on the Cross. When He was crucified, our old nature was crucified and when He rose from the dead, He reconciled us [restored our relationship] back to our heavenly Father. Through Christ, we can have a personal relationship and fellowship with God. We now have salvation, which is deliverance from the power and penalty of sin. This means that we are saved from eternal damnation. This is the good news; through salvation, we have eternal life **(Luke 1:77; Acts 4:12; Romans 1:16; Ephesians 1:13, Galatians 3:2, 5).**

Through the death, burial, and resurrection of Jesus Christ, we received:

1. **Justification,** which is God's act of declaring us "NOT GUILTY" for our SINS **(Romans 4:25; 5:18).**

2. **Propitiation** means the removal of God's punishment for sin through the perfect sacrifice of Jesus Christ. He took our place on the cross **(Romans 3:25).**

3. **Redemption** means Jesus Christ has paid the price, so we can be free from the grip of sin. The price of sin is death; Jesus paid that price (**Romans 3:24; 8:23).** We are reconciled to the Father, which means we have been reunited in relationship with God.

4. **Sanctification** means we become more and more like Jesus Christ through the

work of the Holy Spirit **(Romans 5:2; 15:16).**

CHAPTER 2
NOW THAT YOU ARE A BORN-AGAIN BELIEVER

Because you have made the best decision you will ever make by accepting the Lord and Savior Jesus Christ into your heart, you now have **salvation,** which is complete deliverance from sin and all curses, including death. The word of God says, *"... **if you confess with your mouth Jesus is Lord, and believe in your heart that God***

raised him from the dead, you will be saved." (Romans 10:9)

"Salvation is moral and spiritual. Salvation relates to a deliverance from sin and its consequences and thus guilt, (Rom. 5:1; Heb. 10:22); from the law and its curse (Gal. 3:13; Col. 2:14), from death (1 Pet. 1:3-5; 1 Cor.14:51-56), from judgment (Rom. 5:9; Heb. 9:28), also from fear (Heb. 2:15; 2 Tim. 1:7) and bondage (Tit. 2:11-3; 6; Gal. 5:1). Salvation includes deliverance from sin and all its consequences and positively bestowal of all spiritual blessings in Christ (Eph. 1:3), the gift of the Holy Spirit and the blessedness in the future age (heaven)[1]

Accepting the Lord Jesus Christ into your heart means you have experienced a new "spiritual" birth. Your flesh, which is the earthly part of man, can now live a holy life under the leadership of Jesus Christ and the power of the Holy Spirit. No matter what has happened in your past, your old nature has been crucified and now you have a new life, "a new beginning."

The Spirit from above is the power that affects a new birth. You have been

---

[1] Marshall, I. H., Millard, A. R., J. I. Packer, Wiseman, D.J. *New Bible Dictionary Third Edition.* Grove: Intervarsity Press USA, 1996.

sealed with the Holy Spirit. *"In Him you also trusted, after you heard the word of truth, the gospel of your salvation; in whom also, having believed, you were sealed,"* **(Ephesians 1:8)**. *"Therefore, if anyone is in Christ, he is a new creature; old things have passed away; behold all things have become new"* **(2 Corinthians, 5:17).** It is by faith that you believed that Jesus Christ would come into your heart. *"For it is by grace you have been saved, through faith--and this not from yourselves, it is the gift of God--not by works, so that no one can boast"* **(Ephesians 2:8-9).** It is by faith (belief) that you will live the rest of your "new life" with Jesus as Lord! ***"Faith is the substance of things hoped for, the evidence of things not seen" (Hebrews 11:1).***

Because of your confession of faith, not only are you sealed with the Holy Spirit, you have also been spiritually baptized into the Body of Christ. In **1 Corinthians 12:13,** the Apostle Paul tells us, ***"For we were all baptized by one Spirit into one body-- whether Jews or Greeks, slave or free- -and we were all given the one Spirit to drink."***

Being born-again comes with many benefits! The most important benefit is eternal life! When you accepted the Lord Jesus Christ and repented of your sins, you inherited eternal life. It is only by God's grace, which is His divine love and protection that you are saved! Although we are all eternal beings when we are born, as a born-again believer, when we take our last breath our families can rest assured that our eternity is in heaven. It is those who never accepted Christ into their lives that will spend eternity in hell.

In addition to eternal life, you now have hope and peace. Your life is now whole and complete. Without Jesus Christ in your life, you are incomplete. **God also wants you to be blessed while you are on earth.** In **John 10:10,** Jesus said, *"The thief comes*

only to steal and kill and destroy; I have come that they may have life, and have it to the full." Being born into a "new life" in Jesus Christ brings joy and a peace of mind that no man, woman, or situation can take from you. We don't give anybody our joy because Jesus gave it to us. Jesus came so that we may have peace. In **John 16:33,** Jesus says, ***"I have told you these things so that you know that in the world you will have trouble but in me you may have peace."***

Another benefit of being born-again is the power and authority you have through the Holy Spirit. We will cover more about the Holy Spirit in the next

Chapter.

As a born-again believer, you are now a disciple of Christ. A disciple is "a follower of a teacher." Thus, you are a follower of Jesus Christ, who is our teacher, Lord, and our Savior. As a follower (disciple) of Jesus Christ, we:

(1) Believe His doctrine *(teachings)*
(2) Rest on His sacrifice
(3) Take in His spirit
(4) Imitate His example **(Matthew 10:24; Luke 14:26-27,33; John 6:69; Ephesians, 5:1-2).**

Understanding Our New Life

When we talk about imitating God's example, that includes loving yourself.

God requires that we love our neighbors (those we know and don't know) as we love ourselves. It is so important for you to love you! God expects it! **(Matthew 12:30-31).**

God is Spirit and man is Spirit. In **1 John Chapter 4:13,** John tells us, ***"this is how we know that we live in him and he in us: He has given us his Spirit."*** Humans are comprised of **body** *(SOMA in Greek),* **soul** *(Psyche (in Greek) and* **spirit** *(Pneuma in Greek).*

The Holy Spirit enables us to communicate with God. We "...***worship God in spirit and in truth"* (John**

4:23-24). There are different interpretations on how the spirit and soul operate. The Word of God at times refers to spirit and soul interchangeably. My interpretation of the Scriptures and most biblical scholars believe our soul is the part of us that forms our personality and allows us to function within the psychological sphere. Finally, the physical body, with its five senses, assists us to relate to and communicate with the physical world.

After God created the first man, Adam, from the dust of the earth, God breathed into his nostrils the breath of life. He breathed "spirit" into man. The human spirit was created to be in fellowship with God and to be fed by God. After sin entered the world, our human spirit became lifeless. Sin caused our life to lose our connection (fellowship) with God.

We are spirit beings living temporarily in a human body. Our spirit and soul are the personality and heart of man. That's why it's important to look at life from a spiritual perspective. The world has lost its way because the spirit of darkness (Satan/the devil and the fallen angels) has blinded the eyes and minds of people. As a result, they are making decisions according to their flesh instead of the Holy Spirit. Jesus is the balance and anchor of our life. Just imagine a boat sailing nonstop because it has no direction or anchor; it will eventually crash. The same results occur if you live your life solely on the five senses of sight, smell, hearing, taste, and touch without the filter of the Holy Spirit.

Our Mind

When you are born-again. **1 Corinthians 5:17** says, ***"old things have gone new things have come."*** Although you have accepted Jesus Christ into your heart and you're born-again, it is a process. To walk in the newness of life, you must operate under new godly principles, by new godly rules with new godly designs. The mind is the acting ruling part of us. Renewing of the mind is the renewing of the whole man, for out of it are the *issues of life* **(Proverbs 4:23).** In **Romans 12:2**, Apostle Paul instructs us that we "*Do not conform any longer to the pattern of this world, but be transformed by the renewing of your mind. Then you will be able to test and approve what God's will is--his good, pleasing and perfect will.*" This is one of the biblical principles we live by.

Why is it important to renew our minds daily? Because the "world's system" - the popular culture and manner of thinking is contrary to God. Because of this "rebellion" against God and His teachings, the "world" tempts us to conform to their way of thinking and behaving. The world wants to shape us to its ungodly pattern, and that process must be resisted.

The battle between conforming to the world and being transformed is called *spiritual warfare*. One of the battlegrounds Satan uses is our mind. Christians should not be conformed to this world but rather transformed by the Spirit of God. **Christians must think differently.**

You now may be asking the question, **"How do I change my thinking?" By renewing your mind.** The problem with many

Christians is that they live life based on *feelings*, and/or only concerned about *doing*.

Life based on *doing* says, *"Don't give me your theology; just tell me what to do," "Give me the four points for this and the seven keys for that."* This life of doing will never know the transforming power of God, because it ignores the **renewing of the mind**.

God is never against feeling and doing. He is a God of powerful and passionate feelings, and He commands us to be doers. Yet, feelings and doing are completely insufficient foundations for the Christian life. The first questions cannot be, **"How do I feel?"** or **"What do I do?"** Rather, it must be **"What is true here?**

What does God's Word say?" "What would Jesus do in this situation?"

When you renew your mind with the Word of God, and worship Him, your mind is transforming, which means it's changing and being redesigned with a new attitude! You now have a Christ-like mind! **(Matthew 16:23; Mark 12:30; Romans 8:6).**

You will ultimately stop engaging in your old habits because you no longer have a desire for them. You'll begin to feel uncomfortable around some people you use to hang out with. The good news is your new life is a perfect way to witness and share with your friends, family, and strangers that Jesus Christ changed your life and their lives can be changed as well.

Sanctification is a process of dying to sin and living more in righteousness. This process is carrying on the renewing work, until it is perfected in glory. You will read more about this later in Chapter 10, ***"Spiritual Growth is a Process."***

CHAPTER 3
THE HOLY SPIRIT & BAPTISM

The Holy Spirit is the Spirit of God, the third person of the trinity **(God the Father, God the Son, and God the Holy Spirit—see Appendix for more on the "Trinity.")**

When you accepted the Lord Jesus Christ into your heart and repented of your sins, you were "sealed" with the Holy Spirit. ***"In Him you also***

***trusted, after you heard the word of truth, the gospel of your salvation; in whom also, having believed, you were sealed with the promised Holy Spirit"* (Ephesians 1:8).** After Jesus ascended into heaven after the resurrection, **He sent the Holy Spirit to teach, lead and guide us.** *"But you will receive power when the Holy Spirit comes on you; and you will be my witnesses in Jerusalem, and in all Judea and Samaria, and to the ends of the earth."* **(Acts 1:8).**

It is through the power of the Holy Spirit that we can live a holy life. The Holy Spirit gives us the power to overcome sin. We were born-again by the Spirit (spiritual rebirth), who, leads, guides, and directs our "new life." We are no longer controlled by our flesh (mind, five senses) and our emotions, rather, we are guided by the Holy Spirit. ***"If we live by the Spirit, let us also walk by the Spirit..."* (Galatians 5:17-25).**

Now that the Holy Spirit resides within you, He should dominate your life. However, there is a battle between spirit and your flesh. You will find your old nature trying to dominate your decision-making and make you do the things you use to do before you accepted the Lord. The Holy Spirit should be the president of your life while your flesh should be just a resident. Although it is a daily battle, remember you have the most powerful, God almighty within you. ***"I pray also that the eyes of your heart may be enlightened in order that you may know the hope to which he has called you, the riches of his glorious inheritance in the saints, and his incomparably great power for us who believe. That power is like the working of his mighty strength which he exerted in Christ when he raised him from the dead and seated him at his right hand in the heavenly realms"* (Ephesians 1:18-20).**

Remember, your spirit was reborn, not your flesh. It is a daily battle but remember what the word of God says, "***I can do all things through Christ who strengthens me.***" ***All things are possible through Jesus Christ (Philippians 4:13).***

Although we were sealed with the Holy Spirit, you should seek daily the replenishing power of the Holy Spirit to fill you up. It is the filling of the Holy Spirit that sustains you, gives you power, strength, wisdom, and knowledge. That's why it is important to read the word of God, pray and praise and worship the Lord. The Holy Spirit will not continue to control our life unless we want Him to. ***It's our choice.*** The Holy Spirit cannot dwell in an unclean vessel. We are to ***"...by the mercies of God, you are to present your bodies as a living sacrifice, holy, and acceptable to God, which is your reasonable service. And do not conform to this world, but be transformed by the renewing of your mind, that you may prove what is that good and acceptable and perfect will of God"* (Romans 12:1-2).**

What about Baptism?

If you have already been baptized by immersion, you do not have to be baptized a second time. Baptism is an outward sign of inward grace which symbolizes the death, burial and resurrection of our Lord and Savior, Jesus Christ. Baptism is a public acknowledgement that you believe Jesus died, was buried and on the third day, our heavenly Father raised Him from the dead. Once you stand up from the baptism, you have identified that you have died to sin just as Jesus died as sin for us, and rose again; you have risen and will walk in the newness of life **(Matthew 28:19; Romans 6:4).**

CHAPTER 4
JOY, TRIALS & TRIBULATIONS

You Have Joy That Nobody Can Take from You!

So many people are trying to find what they think is "happiness." They are looking for "love" in all the wrong places. Why? We were created in the image of God and God is Spirit, therefore we are spiritual, too. In their search to fill the "spiritual void," many people end up filling that void with drugs, alcohol, relationships, money, etc., because they don't realize their need to accept Jesus Christ into their lives. They need a relationship with God. Jesus gives us "life" and "light." The Holy Spirit floods our spirit, giving us power. That's why a person who is not born-again (natural man/woman) cannot understand spiritual things **(1 Corinthians 2:14)**.

Only Jesus can give you peace of mind and everlasting joy. The joy of Jesus gives you peace even when you're sad. The joy of Jesus gives you strength when you are weak. Nehemiah, one of the great leaders in the Old Testament, says in **Nehemiah 8:10**, *"Go and enjoy choice food and sweet drinks, and*

send some to those who have nothing prepared. This day is sacred to our Lord. Do not grieve, for the joy of the LORD is your strength." Jesus is the center of your joy. That's why no one can take away your joy because no one can replace the joy that Jesus has given you **(1 Peter 1:8)**.

Trials & Tribulations Will Come

Being a Christian isn't an easy journey. There is a difference between a "church-goer" and a Christian. A "church-goer" may attend church faithfully for many years, but have not been "sanctified and transformed." They are still babies in Christ. Maybe they joined the church, but never joined God by confessing and accepting Jesus Christ as their personal Savior. Maybe they have never been born-again in the spirit and in truth. They may still be walking in the flesh—living according to feelings and allowing their flesh to be the master of their life.

When you are born-again, God should be first in your life. The spirit of God should take a dominant seat and your flesh should take the "backseat" **(John 3:5).** You will experience trials, tribulations, and persecutions. Some of your old friends and even some of your family members will not understand the "new" joy and peace you have. They may even isolate themselves from you. That's all right because Jesus will take care of you and give you the strength you'll need to endure the treatment you may receive. He will also send you spiritual brothers, sisters, and spiritual parents! In **John 15:18,** Jesus says, ***"If the world hates you, keep in mind that it hated me first."***

Remember that the devil is alive, and his job is to whisper things in your ear that are contrary to the will of God. The devil will tempt you, and use people to tempt you to throw you off your square. But thank God, the devil is defeated and has no power **(Philippians 2:5-8).**

"And the devil, who deceived them, was thrown into the lake of burning sulfur, where the beast and the false prophet had been thrown. They will be tormented day and night forever and ever" **(Revelation 20:10)**.

On the contrary, a born-again believer has power to overcome the devil through the Holy Spirit. In **1 John 4:4**, it says, *"You, dear children, are from God and have overcome them, because the one who is in you is greater than the one who is in the world."* Jesus spoke to the disciples and told them, *"I have given you authority to trample on*

snakes and scorpions and to overcome all the power of the enemy; nothing will harm you **(Luke 10:19).** As a disciple of Christ, you have the same power! ***Please note: Jesus uses snakes and scorpions symbolically as your enemies.***

God will send people into your lives who understand "without God, we are nothing." He will send like-minded folks who understand what it means to be a disciple of Christ. For God said, ***"I will neither leave you nor forsake you"*** **(Hebrews 13:5).**

"God is your strength and your refuge, a very present help in

***trouble"* (Psalm 46:1).**

What's so wonderful about being born-again is the assurance of "peace" in your life. It is knowing that whatever you may be going through at home, on your job, or even at church, God is on your side. You will never have to fight another battle alone, because Jesus will fight them for you. In **2 Chronicles 20:15,** God says, ***"...the battle isn't yours, it's God's" (Paraphrased).*** All He asks of you is to have faith and believe in Him, and know that ***"...your help cometh from the Lord."*** Your help doesn't come from the hills; it comes from the Lord **(Psalm 121).** Because ***"you can do all things through***

***Christ that strengthens you," according to God's will* (Philippians 4:13).**

You will experience many challenges that will help you grow spiritually. If you never experience any challenges, you will not grow and gain strength to handle life's difficulties. I am sure you have heard, "no pain, no gain." Just think if you were never challenged to walk as a toddler, you would not be able to walk today. You had to fall to learn how to walk. Trials and tribulations develops your ability to stand strong in the Lord, and to be able to handle adversity because only the spiritually strong will survive in this world. The Word of God tells us that we *"rejoice in our sufferings, because we know that suffering produces perseverance, perseverance, character; and character, hope. And hope does not disappoint us, because God has poured out his love into our hearts by the Holy Spirit, whom he has given us"* **(Romans 5:3-4).**

Every trial and challenge will make you stronger. Why? Because you read the Word of God which feeds your spirit and gives you strength. *"No temptation has seized you except what is common to man. And God is faithful; he will not let you be tempted beyond what you can*

bear. But when you are tempted, he will also provide a way out so that you can stand up under it" (1 Corinthians 10:13).

CHAPTER 5
READ & STUDY THE WORD OF GOD

Read & Study the Word of God

When you read the Bible, you are getting to know God and how powerful and awesome He is. The Bible is the only "living Word," that speaks to your spirit and is healing for your soul. The Bible is "medicine for your soul." All scriptures were ***"inspired by God." (2 Timothy 3:16).*** When you read and study the Bible, God is communicating to you.

Reading and studying the word of God feeds your spirit and soul, which makes you spiritually strong. Just as you need to feed your physical body, your spirit and soul needs to be fed the Word of God. To fight "spiritual warfare," you must become "spiritually strong." Reading the Word of God lets you know just how mighty God is; therefore, you're given the confidence and strength to know that God will take care of you.

It's important to immediately become active in your local church by attending Christian Education Classes, Bible Study, and Sunday Worship service. Identify areas to volunteer and serve. We will cover more on church attendance and serving in Chapter 9.

How to Get Started Reading the Word of God

First, the most effective study Bible I have used and highly recommend is the New International Version Life Application Study Bible (NIV). Start with the Book of Ephesians. As always, write down any questions you have so you can ask your pastor, ministers or other sisters and brothers in Christ at your local church

After you've finished reading Ephesians, read the following books in the order listed:

The Gospels: John, Matthew,

Mark, and Luke. James, Acts, Romans, Galatians, Philippians, 1 & 2 Corinthians, Ephesians, 1 & 2 Peter, 1, 2 & 3rd John, Hebrews, Colossians, 1 & 2 Thessalonians, 1 & 2 Timothy, Titus, Philemon, Jude, and Revelation.

After completing the New Testament, begin reading the Old Testament beginning with Genesis.

The Old Testament views Christ by way of anticipation; the New Testament views Him by way of realization. The Old Testament will truly acquaint you with God and His power. The Old Testament is what Jesus read and is a powerful compilation of God-inspired writings that communicates God's love, wisdom, and greatness! The New Testament books quote many scriptures from the Old Testament. During your Bible reading, you will notice Scripture references to the Old Testament. Turn to those Old Testament references; they were mentioned for reasons you should know about!

CHAPTER 6
HOW TO PRAY

Pray

Praying is essential to your spiritual growth. Just as your physical body needs essential nutrients from the five basic food groups to build a strong and healthy body; your spirit and soul need the essential nutrients necessary to build a strong and healthy spiritual life. Reading the Word of God alone won't make you strong; you need to support your knowledge of the Word with prayer.

You should pray every day. This is called devotion, "devoting" your time to God. Our prayers are not limited to specific times and locations. We should pray without ceasing. We can pray in the car, in the restroom, on the beach; it doesn't matter where you are, you can always find a few minutes to pray. **There are four parts to prayer in which we use the acronym ACTS (1) Adoration, (2) Confession, (3) Thanksgiving and (4) Supplication.**

[2]**ADORATION** (Praise) gives honor to God because of His omnipotent and sovereign rule in all of life.

CONFESSION means to confess your sins to God and ask for forgiveness so

---

[2]Bright, Bill. *Ten Basic Steps Toward Christian Maturity.* San Bernardino: Here's Life Publishers, 1983.

that your heart is clean when you talk to God. ***Psalm 51:6; 16-17; 32; Ezra 9:5.***

THANKSGIVING. Give thanks to God for His goodness and greatness. Thank Him as the supplier of all our needs. ***Psalm 107:1-2; Psalm 136:1; Luke 17:11-19.***

SUPPLICATION means to make an earnest and humble appeal to God, to make requests to God. ***Philippians 4:6-7; Ephesians 6:18-20.***

The prayers of supplication fall into two classifications: (1) intercessory prayer for others, and (2) petition for ourselves.

How to Pray

You should establish some quiet time in the morning or whenever you start your day. Maybe get up before everyone else. Find a place beside your bed or another room. Begin by closing your eyes so that the Lord can speak to you. After silent moments, begin to adore God through praise, **"Father God, you are a mighty God, a Holy God and I praise your Holy name, you are so worthy to be praised."** Then, confess your sins, ask for forgiveness, and ask God to forgive those who have sinned against you. Continue to thank God for His grace and mercy.

Now, it's time to pray for your needs and the needs of others. Practice praying throughout the day. Whenever you can get in a short prayer or praise, do it. Remember you must believe what you are praying for; doubtful prayers are ineffective. Remember to pray, ***"If it is your will, I pray it shall be done."*** There will be times of going through some heavy trials and tribulations where the only thing you can pray is, **"God, give me strength,"** and that's fine, too! God understands and desires sincere, prayers from the heart, rather than legalistic prayers. Remember, you can pray anywhere at any time!

Meditate on "growth and strength scriptures" (Isaiah 40:31; Psalms 20, 23, 27:1-2, 62:1-2, 91, 121:1, 141;

Philippians 4:13, 19; Romans 8:23, 38; 1 Peter 5: 6-7; Hebrews 13:5; 1 John 4:4; Hebrews 13:6, and Matthew 6.

CHAPTER 7
FAITH, OBEDIENCE & WITNESS

Faith

"Faith without works is dead" **(James 2:26).** It isn't enough to just have faith—you need to "act" on your faith. Faith is belief, trust, and total loyalty to God. If you have faith God is going to bless you, you must prepare yourself for the blessing. For example, if you want God to bless you with a job, you must prepare resumes and send them to potential employers. If you want God to bless you with a new car, you need to start saving your money and getting your financial business in order. If you have faith that God is going to deliver you from a situation, you must fast, *(fasting means to abstain. You will find many occasions of fasting in the Old Testament and a few in the New Testament. Fasting should be joined with prayer, so the mind can devote itself with less distraction, so you can focus on God. You can fast from food, TV, Social Media, etc. When you fast, it should be from something you really like which is a real sacrifice. You can fast for ½ day, full day, however long you desire and are physically able.*

You should consult your doctor first if you have any health challenges. Remember, fasting and praying strengthens your relationship with God. I used to fast from food every Wednesday from 9:00am-5:00pm in addition to multiple days with water and fruit. But with the onset of health challenges I could no longer fast from food but could fast from TV, social media, etc., which had more of an impact for me because it is something I enjoy doing and it also commands silence—no noise. Fast according to what works for you.)

You must believe that God is going to answer your prayers, for **"faith is the**

***substance of things hoped for, the evidence of things not seen"* (Hebrews, 11:1).** Although God knows what you need before you ask—He wants you to ask Him. God will bless you according to His will, not yours. Many times, we may pray for the wrong things—and the Holy Spirit intercedes for us. *"In the same way, the Spirit helps us in our weakness. We do not know what we ought to pray for, but the Spirit himself intercedes for us through wordless groans. And he who searches our hearts knows the mind of the Spirit, because the Spirit intercedes for God's people in*

accordance with the will of God' **(Romans 8:26-27).** Remember, God is good, and He only wants what is best for His children. Believe Him with all your heart, and He will reveal Himself to you.

Obedience

Obeying the Word of God is essential to your growth, your strength and anointing. The anointing is the presence of God in your life. The Word of God gives us a set of principles and guidelines for Christian living. ***"Let your light so shine before men that they may see your good works, and glorify your Father which is in heaven"*** **(Matthew 5:16).** Your life should reflect holiness. When you accepted Jesus Christ into your life, you became "sanctified," which means spiritually "set-apart" from the unbelievers. There should be a noticeable difference in your life. *"Therefore, if anyone is in Christ, he is a new creation; the old has gone, the new has come"* **(2 Corinthians 5:17).** As a child of God, you should strive to live a life of holiness. *"Make every effort to live in peace with all men and to be holy, without holiness, no one will see the Lord"* **(Hebrews 12:14).** *"The fruit of your obedience will be evidenced by your, peace, patience, kindness, goodness,*

***faithfulness, gentleness, and self-control"* (Galatians 5:22).**

Transformation is a process. The key is "always striving" to be like Jesus. You were made righteous when Jesus shed His blood and washed away your sins. When you accepted the Lord Jesus into your life, you were "justified," which means, "Just as If You Did Not Sin." Although Jesus was meek and kind, He was also bold and strong. As a born-again believer, you must boldly and confidently stand up for the Gospel of Jesus Christ.

Witness

Now that you are born-again, you

should be eager to share the good news of Jesus Christ—to "witness" to the unsaved and biblically uninformed. God wants us all to share the good news of Jesus Christ, that He died as sin for us and therefore conquered death on the cross. Through His shed blood, Jesus redeemed and saved us. Once a person repents of their sin and accepts Jesus into their hearts, they are God's property and no longer slaves to sin. It is the Christians' responsibility to spread the good news to the unsaved. He didn't save you to keep all His goodness and greatness to yourself! You must share it!

The misunderstanding among many "church-goers" is witnessing is the exclusive responsibility of the preachers and evangelists. However, God commissioned all of His believers to spread the good news. *"…. **Go home to thy friends, and tell them how great things the Lord hath done for you**"* **(Mark 5:19).**

CHAPTER 8
PRAISE, WORSHIP & SPIRITUAL GIFTS

Praise & Worship

The Lord deserves our praise and worship. ***"Praise ye the Lord"* (Psalms 148, 150:1, Revelation 6:13); *"I will bless the Lord at all times; His praise shall continually be in my mouth"* (Psalm 34:1); *"Let them praise His name with dancing"* (Psalm 149:3); and *"O**

clap your hands, all people; shout to God with the voice of Joy" **(Psalm 47:1).**

Praise and worship, takes you to a higher spiritual level. When the praises go up, the blessings come down! Christians should praise God when everything is going well and when we are going through rough times. Praising God while you're going through tests and trials shows the Lord that you love Him unconditionally. It displays your faith; He will bring you out because you know just how great He is! There is healing in our praise and worship. There were times when I was going through some rough situations, and I couldn't wait to get to the house of the Lord to praise and worship God with the saints! There's something about being together, on one accord—I feel better every time! ***"For without faith it is impossible to please Him. For He who comes to God must believe that He is, and that He is a rewarder of those who diligently seek him"* (Hebrews 11:6).**

To "worship God" is to commune, to talk, and to meet with God--your undivided attention is given to Him. There are many ways to worship God: through song, meditation, tithes and offering. Worship is a personal meeting between you and God regardless of who is around you. When you worship God, you are in His presence, and your only focus is God.

Spiritual Gifts

Concerning spiritual gifts, when Jesus ascended into heaven after spending 40 days with His disciples after His resurrection, He sent us the Holy Spirit to empower us. The Lord loved us so much, that He didn't just stop at filling us with the Holy Spirit; He also gave us gifts and talents. All of God's children have one or more gifts. There are different gifts, but the same Spirit. God is the giver of the gifts. There are different kinds of gifts:

- **Word of Wisdom**

- **Word of Knowledge**

- **Prophecy**

- **Tongues**

- **Interpretation**

- **Apostle**

- **Teacher**

- **Encouragement**

- **Leadership**

- **Evangelist**

- **Pastor-Teacher**

- **Faith**

- **Healing**

- **Miraculous power**

- **Service**

- **Discernment**

- **Helps**

- **Administration**

- **Giving**

- **Mercy**

What gifts do you have? Jesus said, ***"If a person being evil knows how to give good gifts unto your children, how much more shall your Father which is in heaven***

***give good things to them that ask"* (Matthew 7:11).** All you need to do is pray and ask God for the gifts(s) you desire. If it is His will for you to have that gift, He will bless you with it. **It's important, however, to make sure you don't praise your gift, but praise the Giver of your gift.** I prayed for the gift of healing and God granted me that gift. I don't boast "I have the gift of healing." However, if someone is sick, I will lay my hands on him or her and pray for their healing. **(Read 1 Corinthians 12, Romans 12, and Ephesians 4).**

CHAPTER 9
CHURCH FELLOWSHIP & SAVED TO SERVE

Why Fellowship is Important

You will begin to hear people say, **"my church family,"** or my **"sister or brother in Christ."** When you are baptized, you are baptized into the "Body of Christ"—a body of born-again believers. It is essential for you to fellowship and worship with God's family. You are now part of the Kingdom of God; you need to begin building relationships with your "church family."

The church is a place where Christians receive spiritual food through preaching, Bible study and Christian education. ***"So, then faith cometh by hearing, and hearing by the word of God" (Romans 10:17).*** As you've read earlier, your spirit and soul must be fed if you are going to survive in this world. If you don't attend church, you'll become spiritually weak and that's when temptation sneaks up on you! The church is like a filling station. When you drive your car all week, by the weekend, it's time to refuel. The same is true for your spirit. When you work all week and deal with the various challenges in life, you need to be "refueled" in the house of the Lord so you can be spiritually strong to handle the next storm. ***"Let us not give up meeting together, as some are in the habit of doing, but let us encourage one another--and all the more as you see the Day approaching"*** **(Hebrews 10:25).** The church is a place where you are equipped with the Word of God, so you can become a bold witness of Jesus Christ, sharing the gospel with the unsaved and biblically uninformed.

The church is also a place where you render service and use the gift(s) that God has given you. Whether it's singing in the choir, helping the pastor, the children's ministry, usher, etc., there's something for you to do. It is fulfilling to render service for the Kingdom of God. It is better to give than to receive.

Saved to Serve

It is truly a blessing to be assured that we have eternal life. When our bodies fall asleep, we will pass on immediately to heaven, reunited with our loved ones who have gone before us. What a blessing and opportunity; but with blessings and opportunities, comes obligations.

First, we have been called to serve God **(Hebrews 9:14, 12:28; Romans 12:1).** Secondly, we all have gifts, talents, and abilities to serve the Kingdom of God **(Colossians 4:17;**

2Titus 4:5).

If our Lord and Savior Jesus Christ did not come to be served but to serve, **SURELY,** we, as grateful, born-again believers, must serve **(Matthew 20:28; Philippians 2:7).** One of the most humbling examples of Jesus' servanthood is when He washed the feet of His disciples. He was teaching them the meaning of servanthood. In **John 13:12-16,** Jesus Christ taught us how to serve one another. He commanded that we do the same. He used the washing of the feet as an illustration. We are expected to serve in the local church--it could be ushering, teaching, singing, outreach, youth, administratively, etc.

There is a place for you to serve in the Kingdom of God through the local church.

CHAPTER 10
SPIRITUAL GROWTH IS A PROCESS

Spiritual Growth

Spiritual growth is a process. You'll never stop growing spiritually. The greatest preachers, evangelists and witnesses for Christ never stop growing. How do we grow? By applying the principles God has laid out for us—the principles that we have summarized in this book. Always strive towards a life of holiness, following God's commands and you will evolve into a strong, bold witness for Christ, and God's blessings will flow upon your life.

Always have faith and remember: God is greater than human words can describe. Make sure you confess your sins unto God. Although your past, present and future sins have been forgiven, confessing your sins relieves your guilt. Remember, we will not be perfect until we meet our Maker. But what we can do is strive for holiness and perfection in all areas of our lives. When we miss the mark, when we fall, we get back up, repent, and move forward in Jesus' name. The shed blood of Christ and the grace & mercy of God helps us get up and try this daily walk again!

Don't measure your growth by comparing yourself with another sister or brother in Christ. God has a plan and a purpose specifically for you. Just pray and trust that God's will be done in your life and watch how God moves in your life. He may not move as fast as you want Him to, but He is always on time. Continue to be obedient in prayer, fasting and fellowship. You have the most powerful One on your side—and knowing that, you are ***more than a conqueror!* (Romans 8:28)**

ABOUT THE AUTHOR

Rev. Linda Seatts-Ogletree is an ordained Christian minister who has served in ministry for over 20 years. She is Assistant Pastor of Commonwealth of Faith Church under the leadership of Pastor Torian Bridges.

She is founder and president of **Faith and Hope Ministries, International**, a non-denominational international outreach and discipleship teaching ministry, empowering all of God's children to apply biblical teachings to their daily lives. Her powerful life application teachings are transformative. Rev. Seatts-Ogletree is also the president of **Release & Refresh Women's Empowerment Series, Inc.,** a ministry ordained to improve the mental, spiritual, and physical health of women and girls through workshops, seminars, classes, and conferences.

She hosts a weekly radio show on Wednesdays from 11:30am-12:00pm on

1440AM WMKM. Through her **Seeds of Hope** radio broadcast, she disciples, empowers, and sows' seeds of hope. In 2001 Rev. Seatts-Ogletree planted Center of Hope Ministries, International, an urban non-denominational evangelistic and discipleship ministry she pastored for six years.

Rev. Seatts-Ogletree earned a Bachelor of Arts degree in Business Administration/Marketing; a Master of Arts in Christian Ministry, with a concentration in missions and English Bible from Ashland Theological Seminary; and a Master of Arts in Dispute Resolution from Wayne State University. She is also Adjunct Faculty at Ashland Theological Seminary and formerly at Wayne State University.

She has preached the gospel across the world with a fervent desire to see everyone saved and live in the freedom Jesus Christ so passionately gave us. Along with preaching the gospel, Rev. Seatts-Ogletree is a human and civil rights advocate.

She is the best-selling author of ***Did I Say That? How to Communicate in Everyday Life***, and will publish the revised edition of ***The Truth about the Superior Lie: Resurrecting the Lives of African-Americans Crucified by the Lie in*** February 2018. She is happily married to Richard and enjoys spending time with their children and grandchildren.

Feel free to contact Rev. Seatts-Ogletree at
info@faithhopeministries.org.

Visit our websites:
www.commonwealthoffaith.org
www.faithhopeministries.org
www.releaserefreshwomenempowermentseries.org

Appendix

The Holy Trinity

Although the word "trinity" isn't literally found in the Holy Bible, trinity means "tri-unity" or "three-in-oneness!" It is used to summarize the teaching of Scripture that God is in three persons, [Father, Son, & Holy Spirit] yet one God. [i]

Because God lives outside of time as we know it, it's hard for us to intellectualize how there can be three persons and one God when each is God!

> *Then God said, "**Let us make mankind in our image, in our likeness**, so that they may rule over the fish in the sea and the birds in the sky, over the livestock and all the wild animals, and over all the creatures that move along the ground." Genesis 1:26*

Notice it reads, "Let us" which indicates the community of Father, Son & Holy Spirit in the very beginning of creation.

> ***As soon as Jesus was baptized, he went up out of the water. At that moment heaven was opened, and he saw the Spirit of God descending like a dove and lighting on him. And a voice from heaven said, "This is my Son, whom I love; with him I am well pleased." Matthew 3:16-17.***

Notice what happens after John the Baptist baptizes Jesus! The Holy Spirit descended like a dove; and God the Father spoke, ***"this is my son in whom I am well pleased." (The Trinity- God the Father, God the Son, and God the Holy Spirit).*** It's important to understand that there is one God in three persons.

---

[i] Grudem, Wayne. Systematic Theology: An Introduction to Biblical Doctrine: Zondervan; Grand Rapids: 2000

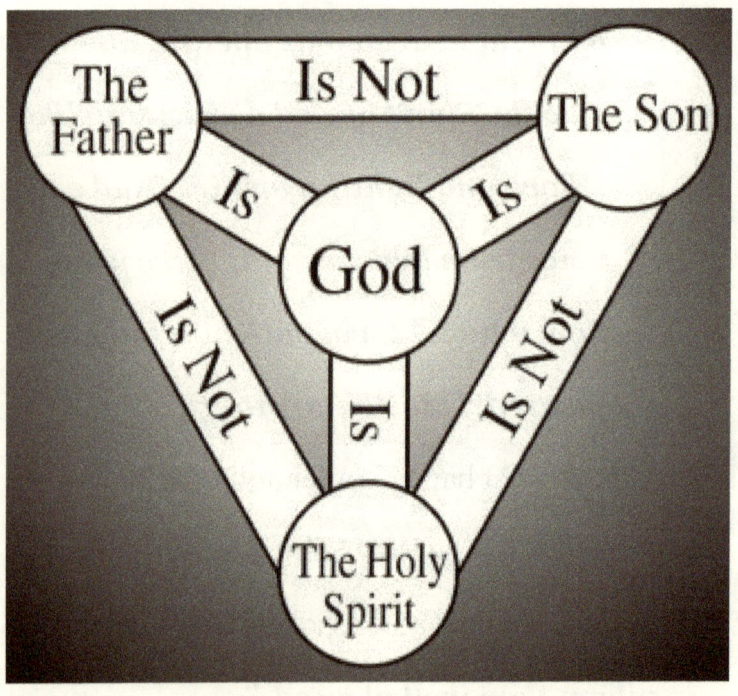

Bibliography

Bright, Bill. *Ten Basic Steps Toward Christian Maturity.* San Bernardino: Here's Life Publishers, 1983.

Grudem, Wayne. *Systematic Theology: An Introduction to Biblical Doctrine.* Grand Rapids: Zondervan, 2000.

International Bible Society, Zondervan. *Life Application Study Bible. New International Version.* Carol Stream: Tyndale House Publishers, Inc., 1995 and Grand Rapids: Zondervan, 1984.

Marshall, I. H., Millard, A. R., J. I. Packer, Wiseman, D.J. *New Bible Dictionary Third Edition.* Grove: Intervarsity Press USA, 1996.